DEFENDING

Gill Harvey

Designed by Stephen Wright
Photographs by Chris Cole
Illustrations by Bob Bond

Edited by Cheryl Evans; Cover Design by Tom Lalonde;
Digital Imaging by John Russell; Consultant: John Shiels,
Bobby Charlton International Soccer Schools Ltd.

Library photographs: Allsport UK; Cover photograph: Alex Livesey/Getty Images
With special thanks to soccer players Carl Brogden, John Cox, Nathan Miles, Andrew Perkin,
Leanne Prince, Peter Riley, Ben Tipton, Neil Wilson and to their coach, Bryn Cooper

CONTENTS

ABOUT DEFENDING

When your team loses the ball, you need to get it back as quickly as possible. This is what defending is all about. When the other team has the ball, you are defending, even if you play in an attacking position. Defending well is every player's responsibility, and it plays a big part in winning matches.

A LOOK AT THE PITCH

Here you can find out the names of the different parts of the pitch that you will come across as you read. Although you can defend anywhere on the pitch, some areas are mentioned more than others because you need to defend more urgently when the other team gets close to your goal.

Good defending uses a mixture of individual skills, team skills and tactics. This book covers all of them. It also looks at the roles of players who are specifically defenders, such as centre halves and full backs.

The 'far' post is the goal-post furthest from the ball.

The goal area is the box around the goal. The goalkeeper usually tells other players what to do in this area.

Goal-line

The penalty area.

The 'near' post is the goal-post nearest the ball at any time.

Half-way line

THE DEFENSIVE STANCE

When you adopt the 'defensive stance', it is almost like being ready to pounce. You don't have the ball so you don't have to worry about controlling it – you can concentrate on your movements instead.

Use your arms for balance.

You should crouch as low as you can so that you are ready to spring.

Your weight should be over your toes so that you can move quickly into action.

USEFUL SOCCER PHRASES

★ 'Reading the game' means being able to work out how the game is going, anticipate attackers' moves, see what help your team-mates need and go to help them.
★ 'Winning the ball' means taking the ball off another player by tackling or intercepting it.

AN IMPORTANT RULE: STAYING GOAL-SIDE

One of the main rules for defending players is to get into a goal-side position and stay there. This means placing yourself between attackers and your goal, never between attackers and the ball. This point is made frequently throughout the book.

Direction of goal

This is the correct direction to take to reach a goal-side position.

If the defender runs to intercept and fails, he gives the attackers a very big advantage.

You may think it makes sense to get between the ball and your opponent, but then you can't see what he's doing.

If he does receive the ball, you have to chase him up the field and he is free to run straight towards your goal.

If you are in a goal-side position, you are able to watch and anticipate the attacker's moves from behind.

Although he is likely to receive the ball successfully, you are in a position to stop his attack and challenge him.

HOW TO MEASURE

For many of the games and exercises in this book, you need to measure out an area to do them in. Measurements are given in metres (m) and feet (ft). 1m (3ft) is about one big stride, so you can measure by counting out your strides.

GOAL-SIDE GAME

This game is for two players, an attacker (A) and a defender (D). Mark out a pitch 20m (60ft) long and 10m (30ft) wide.

20m (60ft)   10m (30ft)

A tries to dribble down the pitch. D tries to stop him by staying goal-side, without tackling.

Whenever A gets goal-side of D, he gets a point. At the end, swap roles. See who scores the most.

PRIORITIES IN DEFENCE

The main purpose of a defender or defending team is to stop opponents from attacking. There are many ways to do this, depending on how urgent the situation is. Here, you can find out about the most important things you need to know. They are all covered in detail later in the book.

YOUR TOP PRIORITY

If your opponents reach the defending third, they are in a very strong position. You must stop them from scoring.

First, help your goalkeeper to block any shots at goal. Next, clear the ball out of the danger area – 'if in doubt, get the ball out.'

Here, a defender stops a shot and clears the ball.

CHALLENGING FOR THE BALL

Whatever the situation, someone must try to win the ball back. This responsibility passes from player to player, so everyone must be ready to take on the challenge if the ball comes his way.

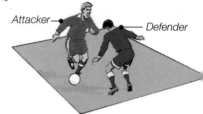

Attacker — — *Defender*

You can challenge by putting pressure on the player with the ball.

If your opponent makes a mistake, you or a team-mate can intercept the ball.

As a last resort, you can challenge your opponent directly with a tackle.

DELAYING YOUR OPPONENTS

A very important way of preventing an emergency situation from happening is to delay your opponents as long as possible.

Delay allows members of your own team to get into a stronger position, which may stop the attack from getting any further.

This player jockeys to give his team-mate time to get into position.

AWARENESS AND TEAM WORK

Even if one player's skills are very good, he will not stand a very big chance of challenging for the ball successfully if his team is not working with him.

Each player has a part to play in making it difficult for the other team to progress up the field. To do this you need to communicate well.

Everyone needs to be aware of where the ball is, but not everyone should crowd around it.

All players should be aware of what the attackers are doing, especially the players they are marking.

The defenders in this team are marking attackers very closely.

Each player needs to understand his team's formation and how his own position works within it.

DEFENCE INTO ATTACK

If you only think about stopping the other team from scoring, you are less likely to score yourself. A good defence makes the whole team strong, but it should always be used as a springboard for attack.

Think positively all the time so that you can turn defensive situations into an attack as soon as you get the chance.

This team gains possession in the defending third, then sends the ball quickly up the pitch.

STAR DEFENDER

German player Dieter Eilts is a good example of a defender who can read the game well, then act courageously to turn defence into attack.

JOCKEYING

Jockeying is one of the most important defending skills. It means delaying your opponent's attack by getting in his way. This allows your team-mates to get into a position where they can help you to challenge. If you do this effectively, you may also pressurize your opponent into making a mistake.

MOVING INTO POSITION

If your opponent is approaching your goal you need to close in on him quickly, but not too quickly. If you are going too fast he will be able to judge your run and dodge round you easily.

The defender watches the ball carefully.

Direction of goal

Once you are close to the attacker, hold off slightly. You should be close enough to touch him, but if you get much closer it will be easy for him to dash round you.

Adopt the 'defensive stance'. If your weight is over your knees, you are in a strong position to challenge.

Make sure you stay goal-side. If the attacker gets past you, he has beaten you. You will no longer be able to jockey.

MAINTAINING THE PRESSURE

As well as delaying your opponent, try to force him into a weaker position. First of all, try to work out which is his weaker side – if he usually uses his right foot to dribble or kick, he is weak on his left side.

This player jockeys on the left.

Cover your opponent to the front and to one side so that it is difficult for him to turn.

The attacker is forced into the side-lines.

If you jockey on his strong side, he will only be able use his weak side, so he may make a mistake.

Here, the attacker loses the initiative.

Once you have your opponent under pressure, watch for opportunities to win the ball.

PREVENTING A FULL TURN

If the attacker is still facing away from your goal when you reach a jockeying position, you have a big advantage. The best thing you can do is prevent him from turning.

1. Jockey on his stronger side, getting close up behind him. You must stay goal-side, so don't come round to his front.

Direction of goal

Direction of goal

2. If you prevent him from turning like this, you will probably force him to pass the ball back.

Direction of goal

3. If he passes back, he may turn and run into space behind you. Stick with him and stay goal-side.

ZIGZAG JOCKEYING EXERCISE

This exercise helps you to work on speed and a good defensive stance. Any number can join in, as long as you work in pairs. Mark out a row of zigzags about 30m (90ft) long and 5m (15ft) wide. One end of the row is the defender's goal. In each pair, decide on an attacker and a defender.

Defender's goal

5m (15ft)

30m (90ft)

When this pair is half-way, the next pair starts.

1. The attacker dribbles towards the 'goal', going from marker to marker, as the defender jockeys him. The defender must stay goal-side all the time.

2. The defender can't tackle, but he scores a point for intercepting the ball if the attacker loses control. The attacker scores if he dodges round the defender. At the end of the row, swap roles and start again.

For a link to a website where you can find out how to jockey your opponent, go to www.usborne-quicklinks.com

CHALLENGING

When you challenge, you make a direct attempt to get the ball back from your opponents. The most direct way to challenge is to tackle, but it is not always the best. If you can intercept the ball instead, do so, because this will leave you with more control.

Defender

APPROACHING AN OPPONENT

You usually move in to challenge when your opponent is about to receive a pass. Always get into a goal-side position.

The defender should not run right to the back of his opponent in the direction of the curved arrow.

Approach your opponent at an angle. If you are directly behind him, he can easily run out to the side.

Don't get in too close to him, as he may be able to dodge round you.

Judge your speed carefully. If you come in too slowly he may run on. If you are too fast, you have less control.

This defender has come in too fast and too close. He is off balance.

If the defender approaches in this direction, he will be able to challenge the attacker.

Direction of goal ⬆

INTERCEPTING

Intercepting is the best way to win the ball back. Your opponents are usually moving in the wrong direction, and you are more balanced than if you tackle. This means that you have time and space to launch an attack.

Wait, then intercept later.

Be patient and wait for a chance to intercept. Attackers may make mistakes under pressure.

You must be on your toes and ready to dash around your opponent from your goal-side position.

If you don't think you can intercept successfully, hold on to your goal-side position instead.

TIMING A DIRECT CHALLENGE

If you are close to your opponent, you will probably need to tackle in order to win the ball. In judging your tackle, the most important factor is timing.

One of the main rules of timing is to watch the ball, not the player. This way, you won't be fooled by his movements. Wait until he is off balance, for example when he is turning or half-turned, then move in quickly to steal the ball. You can find out more about tackling techniques on pages 10-11.

As this player turns with the ball, the defender dashes across the front of him and pushes the ball away.

INTERCEPTING EXERCISE

This exercise is to help you develop your agility and speed at intercepting. Play in threes (A, B and D). Mark out a 10m (30ft) square. A and D stand in the middle of it, B along one edge. The direction of play is towards A and D.

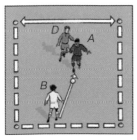

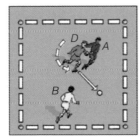

D scores a point if he stops A.

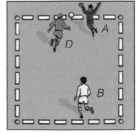

D stands goal-side of A. B passes towards them. D must judge whether to intercept or stay goal-side.

If D intercepts, he scores a point and passes the ball back to B before A can challenge him.

If A gets the ball, D tries to stop him reaching the far side of the square before B can count to ten.

A scores a point for turning and reaching the other side. After five goes, swap your roles around.

TACKLING SKILLS

To tackle well you need a combination of good technique and plenty of determination. You need to tackle cleanly to avoid giving away a foul, and whenever possible you need to keep possession of the ball, too. These are the main techniques that you need to learn.

FRONT BLOCK TACKLE

Watch the ball, not your opponent. With your weight forward, go into the tackle with your whole body.

Use the inside of your tackling foot to make contact with the middle of the ball.

If you watch your opponent instead of the ball, you may be tricked by a feinting move.

The impact of the tackle can often trap the ball between your foot and your opponent's foot. If this happens, drop your foot down and try to flick or roll the ball up over your opponent's foot.

TACKLING FROM OTHER ANGLES

You can use a block tackle to challenge from the side, but not from behind as this is a foul.

Turn your whole body towards your opponent so that all your strength is behind the tackle. Use the side of your tackling foot as you would if you were face on. Lean into your opponent, but don't push.

BLOCK TACKLE PRACTICE

In pairs, mark out a 10m (30ft) line. Start at either end. One player dribbles, the other challenges.

10m (30ft)

The dribbler tries to get to the end of the line, while the challenger tries to win the ball from him. Whoever succeeds scores a point.

SLIDING TACKLES

Sliding tackles are a last resort. You should only use them in a real emergency, for several reasons. You will probably not gain possession of the ball, you are out of the game until you get up again, and you may also give away a foul.

Approach from the side. Keep your eyes on the ball and slide your tackling leg forward to push the ball as far as possible.

This player uses the leg furthest from his opponent to hook the ball away from him.

If you kick the ball and not your opponent, you will not be penalised if he has to jump over you.

After tackling, get up quickly. This is easier if you tackle with the leg furthest from your opponent.

LEARNING TO SLIDE TACKLE

Until you are sure of your technique, it is best to practise sliding tackles without an opponent, as you are less likely to hurt someone. Try this practice with a friend.

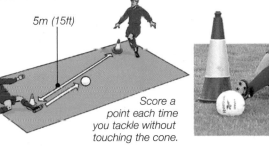

5m (15ft)

Score a point each time you tackle without touching the cone.

Place two obstacles 5m (15ft) apart (they needn't be cones) and put the ball close to one of them. These are your 'opponents'. Each of you starts next to an obstacle.

One of you runs up and slides the ball away, trying not to touch the obstacle. The other collects the ball and puts it next to his own obstacle. He slides it back.

KEEPING IT CLEAN

Tackling your opponent from behind, kicking him or tripping him are fouls which lead to a direct free kick, or a penalty if you are in the penalty area. To avoid fouling, remember these tips:
★ Keep your eyes on the ball, not on your opponent.
★ Be patient. If you wait for the right moment to tackle, you are more likely to do so cleanly.
★ Never tackle half-heartedly. If your weight is not behind the tackle, you may be unbalanced, and you could hurt yourself as well as your opponent.

PLAYING SAFE

Usually, you are defending whenever your team loses the ball. However, when the ball is in your defending third, you may need to play defensively even when your team has possession.

Here, a team-mate collects a long pass up the field.

PLAYING OUT OF THE DEFENSIVE THIRD

If you have possession of the ball in the defending third, for example from a goal kick, it is crucial not to lose it. Defenders must get the ball up the field into safety.

Never dribble out of the defending third. Any attacker who wins the ball may be able to shoot.

This attacker wins the ball and can now go for goal.

You can pass between yourselves at the back until you get a good opportunity to pass up the field.

When you pass up the field, send the ball as far as you can, to a team-mate if possible.

BACK-PASSES

A 'back-pass' usually means passing the ball back to the goalkeeper. If you want to pass up the field but find yourself surrounded, this is sometimes your only option.

1. Never pass across your goalmouth, as this may give your opponents a chance to run in and shoot.

2. Don't pass back to the goalkeeper if he is under pressure. It is better to kick the ball out of play.

3. Play the ball low, to the goalkeeper's kicking foot. This makes it easier for him to control.

BACK-PASS RULES

There are particular rules for back-passes to bear in mind.
★ If you kick the ball to him, the goalkeeper can't pick it up. He has to kick it instead.
★ The goalkeeper can pick up any back-pass that you make with your head, chest or thighs.
★ The goalkeeper can pick up any accidental back-pass.

GOING FOR TOUCH

'Going for touch' means sending the ball off the pitch on purpose as an emergency move. The other team still has the initiative because they get the corner or throw-in, but it can stop them from scoring while your team uses the time to strengthen its position.

1. Going for touch usually involves a split-second attack on the ball, pushing it away from your opponent's feet. To avoid giving away a corner, try to send the ball into the side-lines rather than behind the goal-line.

Sideline

Here, a throw-in gives defenders time.

2. If you have played for touch, your whole team must make use of the time you have gained to run into a stronger position.

THE PENALTY AREA: GETTING INTO POSITION

In your penalty area, you should do everything you can to prevent a goal, but don't take any risks.

This player jockeys while other defenders get into position.

Position yourself to stop any shots, as this player is doing.

Keep a close guard on other attackers close to the penalty area.

Help your goalkeeper by listening to him carefully.

You should still try to delay your opponent for as long as possible.

Don't try to tackle the player with the ball unless you are sure of success.

Help the goalkeeper by getting into a position to block any shots at goal.

If you get a touch of the ball, use it to clear the ball out of danger (see page 14).

CLEARING THE BALL

In the defending third, and even more so in the penalty area, you need speed, courage and aggression to clear the ball out of danger. First of all, you must reach it before an attacker gets to it and then you must go for the ball and attack it fearlessly.

SPEED, HEIGHT AND DISTANCE

Volleys are good for sending the ball high.

You must get to the ball quickly. When you get to it, aim for the wings. Attackers are more likely to come up the centre of the field.

Send the ball as high as you can. This gives your team time to get into position, even if it doesn't go very far.

It is even better to send the ball high and a long way. Use a powerful kick such as a lofted drive to get height and distance.

DEFENSIVE HEADERS

As for any header, keep your mouth shut and your eyes open.

Take the ball as early as possible. This will automatically send your header higher and further.

Brace your legs and take off on one leg, springing at the ball and arching your back in the air.

Aim to hit the ball from underneath so that your forehead sends it high over attackers' heads.

If you need to, turn your head as you make contact to send the ball away from the penalty area.

CLASHES IN THE AIR

The penalty area is often crowded, so clashes with attackers in the air are bound to happen. Success in this situation requires courage and dominance, so take the initiative. Attacking the ball aggressively actually gives you greater control.

Communicate with your goalkeeper and team-mates to avoid clashing with them as well as with attackers.

Timing is crucial. Try to jump before the attacker. He may then push you up further from underneath.

Be careful not to give away a free kick. Don't push the attacker with your arms.

CLEARANCE PRACTICE

This practice is best for seven players in the positions shown, but you can vary it. The two Ws stand on either side of the penalty area and everyone else in the goalmouth.

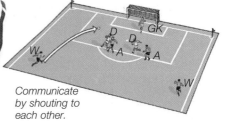

Communicate by shouting to each other.

One of the Ws sends a high pass into the goalmouth. The GK and Ds have to communicate quickly and decide who will go for it.

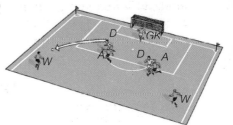

If a D gets to the ball, he should try to direct it out to a W with a header, lofted drive or volley. If an A gets to the ball, he tries to shoot.

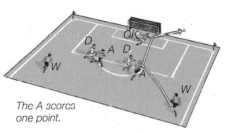

The A scores one point.

Whoever gets the ball first scores a point. Ds score two for getting the ball out of the penalty area, As two for scoring. Swap roles after five passes.

STAR HEADER

When you watch professional players, see how they approach the ball in the penalty area. You will see that they are never afraid to leap into the air and go for the ball, and they are not afraid of making physical contact with other players.

Here, Spanish midfielder 'Felipe' Minambres leaps for the ball in a match against Korea.

For links to websites with animations, tips and training drills on heading, go to www.usborne-quicklinks.com

SUPPORT PLAY

Individual defending skills are very important, but in order to win matches you must also work well as a team. While one player challenges for the ball, everyone else should try to stop other attackers from getting into a strong position.

Here, one player challenges while the others close down on opponents.

CLOSING DOWN SPACE

Your opponents will try to spread the game out and make holes in your defence by running into space. 'Closing down space' means moving to cover attackers who are free, while one or two players move in to cover the player with the ball.

Direction of goal

Everyone should run into a goal-side position. Make sure you cover all the players who are likely to receive a pass.

Try to move up the field together. Working well with each other makes it much harder for attackers to find space in between you.

The result should be that the attackers' route is blocked, and that they have nowhere to pass the ball.

COVERING A CHALLENGE

If you are close to a player challenging for the ball, you must give him all the help you can to stop the attack. If the attacker gets past him, you should be ready to take up the challenge. Here, you can see a two-on-two situation where two defenders mark two attackers.

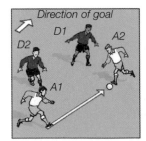

As one attacker (A1) passes to the other (A2), one defender (D1) moves in to challenge him.

The other defender (D2) moves back at an angle so that he can still keep an eye on A1.

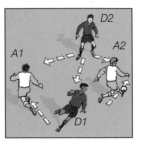

D1 now has cover behind him if he loses the challenge, but A1 is still being marked by D2.

MARKING

Good marking is one of the keys to a solid defence. When and who you mark may depend on your marking system (see pages 18-19) but the basic principles stay the same.

This player is in a position to see the ball and his opponent.

Direction of goal

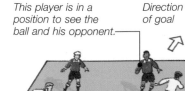

You need to be goal-side and at the correct angle from your opponent so that you can watch him and the game at the same time.

This player cannot see the ball.

If you mark directly behind your opponent, you may block your own view of the game. It is also difficult to intercept any passes to him.

This attacker manages to get around the defence.

If you turn to watch the ball without keeping an eye on the player you are marking, he may be able to sneak around you.

JUDGING YOUR DISTANCE

To judge the right distance to keep, work out how fast your opponent is. Do this by watching him carefully at the start of the game. If he is slower than you, stay quite close to him. You may be able to intercept passes coming his way.

By marking tightly, this defender can dash round the attacker.

If your opponent is faster than you, stay at about arm's length from him. If you get too close, he may be able to dodge around you when he receives the ball.

This defender is ready to challenge.

For links to websites where you can see turns and tricks your opponents might use, go to **www.usborne-quicklinks.com**

17

MARKING SYSTEMS

A marking system is a way of organising your team so that everyone knows who should be covering which attacker. These are the systems used most often, which can be adapted to fit the strengths and weaknesses of your team.

MAN-TO-MAN MARKING

When your team marks man-to-man, a specific defender marks each of the attackers from the other team. They watch this attacker throughout the game and stay goal-side of him whenever necessary.

Here, the defenders are moving into position.

Playing man-to-man works well in the defending third, as long as you have some spare defenders to put the attackers under pressure. Never let just one player mark the opponent who has the ball.

As the play moves across the pitch towards the penalty area, the marking defenders stay with the same player, keeping goal-side and marking tightly. This makes it difficult for the attackers to shoot.

ZONAL MARKING

In zonal marking, you are responsible for an area or zone instead of one player. This area depends on the position you are playing, but not too strictly. As you move up and down the pitch, your area moves with you. Usually, you mark anyone who comes within 5-10m (15-30ft) of you.

In this example of how the zonal system works, an attacker (A) moves across the defence.

D1 covers the player until he moves out of his area, when D2 covers him instead.

The advantage of this is that D1 has not left a big space behind him for attackers to fill.

MIXING SYSTEMS

Many professional teams don't work with just one system. Often, they mix different systems to make the most of their skills. This takes a lot of discipline and organization to put into practice effectively.

When one player in the other team is very skilful, one defender might mark him man-to-man while the others mark zonally, as this picture shows.

Some teams play zonally in the attacking third and midfield, then use a man-to-man system in defence.

One defender marks this fast winger closely, while the other defenders mark zonally.

You can also mark different players at different times as a looser man-to-man system.

USING A SWEEPER

Whichever system you use, it is too risky to allow a one-on-one situation to develop in the defending third. To stop this from happening, you can use a 'sweeper', who doesn't mark anyone (see pages 20-21). He stays at the back and 'sweeps up' attackers who get past the main defence.

FINDING THE BEST SYSTEM

There is no 'best system' which works for every team in every situation. These are the factors which are important.
★ Whatever system you use, the whole team must fully understand it. Each player must know exactly what he is supposed to do.
★ Try to find out about your opponents and about their strengths and weaknesses. If they have some good players, make sure they are well marked.
★ Think about the skills of your own team - for example, you might put a row of strong players to mark zonally at the back, and you wouldn't place a weak player man-to-man against a strong opponent.

This sweeper gets into a good position to challenge an attacker who has broken through the defence.

Direction of goal

TEAM FORMATIONS

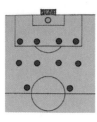

Along with a marking system, each professional team has a formation. A formation is almost like a map of the positions that the players stick to during the game. It can be different each time a team plays, though teams often use the one they feel most confident with.

HOW IS A FORMATION BUILT?

A strong formation always has a strong defence. A team is usually built up solidly with a strong group of defenders at the back for the attackers to rely upon. The idea is that if the other team can't score, they can't win. This way of thinking, however, can lead to play that is too defensive and to games which end in a draw. To win, teams also need to give the midfield and attackers support and freedom to push forward and score, so modern formations are designed for this as well.

FOUR-FOUR-TWO

In some countries, the 4-4-2 formation is used more than any other formation. After the goalkeeper, it has a line of four defenders, then four in midfield and two in attack.

The two wingers are in a good defensive position, but they can also run down into attack when they get the chance.

The midfielders have a lot of work to do in attack and in defence.

The back four in this formation provide a firm line of defence.

FOUR-THREE-THREE

This formation is similar to the 4-4-2 formation. It has a goalkeeper, four defenders, three midfielders and three attackers. The advantage of this is that there is more emphasis on attack, but the problem can be that the midfield is not strong enough to push the ball forward in the first place.

Having less midfielders makes the defence weaker.

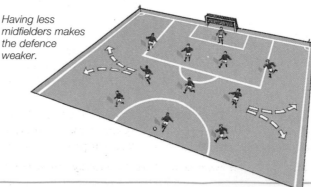

THE SWEEPER FORMATION

Using a sweeper changes a formation at the back. Traditionally, the system is based on a five-man defence. The usual line of four is backed up by a 'spare' man or sweeper.

This formation gives a very secure defence. However, with so many players at the back, a team using it may find it difficult to attack.

Another version has more players in attack. It uses the usual back four, but one player drops back when necessary to play sweeper.

Direction of goal

There are rarely more than three attackers in an opposing team, so the sweeper is still a 'spare' player.

OTHER FORMATIONS

There are many other combinations which teams can try. This is an example. It is based on the 4-4-2 formation, but it is a lot more flexible.

The 'link' players need to be very fit.

This system has a 'link' player between the defence and midfield, and between the midfield and attack. In defence, the 'link' is similar to a sweeper but in front of the line of backs instead of behind them.

In this system, players' roles are less clearly defined. They must all be able to vary their game.

WHICH IS BEST?

Each formation has its advantages and teams tend to get used to playing in one way. Many European teams, for example, use a sweeper. The following factors make a difference when you are deciding which to use.

★ Don't try to fit players to a formation which doesn't suit them. Choose one which suits their skills.
★ If you use a very traditional formation, your game may be too easy for your opponents to read.

★ If you use a new, flexible formation, you must all be able to read the game well, and you must also be very fit.
★ Make sure you have a strong defence. If it is weak, you may lose even if your attackers are good.

For a link to a website where you can find out more about different team formations, go to **www.usborne-quicklinks.com**

THE OFFSIDE RULE

The offside rule can sometimes be very useful for defenders, as attackers who are caught in this position have an indirect free kick awarded against them. Here you can find out about how the rule works and the best way for defenders to use it.

OFFSIDE

To be penalized for offside, an attacker must be in your half of the pitch and there must be fewer than two defenders between him and the goal-line. One of these defenders can be the goalkeeper. It is not always illegal to be offside, but it is in any of these cases:

1. A player can only be called offside when the ball is played, not when it is received.

2. Offside should be called if a player's offside position gives him an advantage, for example a chance to shoot.

3. If a player is offside and obstructs a defender to stop him from reaching the ball, he should be penalized.

LEGAL POSITIONS

An attacker will not be penalized for offside in any of these situations:

1. If one of the last defenders is level with him when the ball is passed. To be offside he must be closer to the goal-line.

2. If he receives the ball directly from a goal-kick, corner or throw-in. If he receives it indirectly, he is offside.

3. If he runs into an offside position after the ball has been played, or if he dribbles into an offside position.

4. If he is offside, but not interfering with play at all – for example, if he is on the other side of the pitch or if he is lying injured.

USING OFFSIDE IN DEFENCE

You may see professional defenders trying to place an attacker offside by moving up the pitch together, just at the point when another attacker passes to him. Here you can see how this 'trap' works.

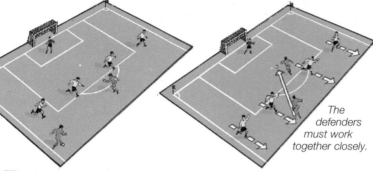

The defenders must work together closely.

The back line of defenders see that an attacker is about to receive a pass.

They all move up the pitch just before or just as the pass is made.

DISADVANTAGES OF USING OFFSIDE

A big problem with using offside is that you depend upon the referee. If he does not call offside, you leave your defence in a very weak position. Also, the trap may not work. If an attacker manages to dribble past you instead of passing, he can go straight for goal.

OFFSIDE QUIZ

Which of these situations show a player in an offside position? Think carefully before you decide. The answers are on page 32.

1.

2.

3.

4.

This attacker fools the defence by dribbling past them instead of passing.

The defenders expect the ball to be passed to this player.

The defenders have all moved up, so it will be difficult for them to help the goalkeeper defend against the attacker.

*For a link to a website where you can see an animated guide to being offside, go to **www.usborne-quicklinks.com***

DEFENSIVE POSITIONS

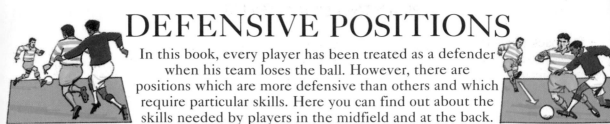

In this book, every player has been treated as a defender when his team loses the ball. However, there are positions which are more defensive than others and which require particular skills. Here you can find out about the skills needed by players in the midfield and at the back.

PLAYING CENTRE HALF

The centre half's number one job is to stop the other team from scoring.

★ You mustn't be afraid to challenge for the ball and tackle. It helps if you are strong.

★ You need to be able to head the ball well.

★ You need to read the game from the back and communicate well with your team-mates.

★ If you move forward when your team attacks, you must be able to move goal-side quickly if your opponents counter-attack.

Main area of responsibility:

★ *Typical situation: The centre half sees an attack coming up the field. He reads the situation and gets into position.*

Direction of goal

When the attacker kicks the ball, the centre half is ready to clear it out of danger.

PLAYING SWEEPER

In some formations, a centre half drops back to play sweeper (see page 21), so the skills needed are similar. These are the main differences:

★ You have to cover the whole of the area behind the back four, so you must be quick and agile.

★ You must be an even better judge of the game, as you are further back than a centre half and in a position to spot any danger.

Main area of responsibility:

★ *Typical situation: A centre half and a full back are challenging an attack up the wing.*

The sweeper sees an attacker moving out to receive a pass, so he moves to cover him.

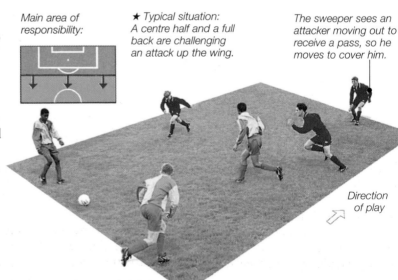

Direction of play

PLAYING FULL BACK

A full back plays in defence, but on the wing. This is a varied role. You need lots of different skills to play it well.

★ Like a centre half, you need to be aggressive and strong to clear the ball out of danger.

★ Because you are on the wing, you need to be fast, fit and able to make runs up and down the pitch to support the attack as well as the defence.

★ You need to be good at jockeying attackers on the wing to give other defenders time to get into position.

Main area of responsibility:

Direction of goal

Full back

Centre half

Midfielder

★ *Typical situation: The full back sprints to jockey an attacker moving up the wing.*

Once he has enough cover, he tackles and passes to a midfield player.

PLAYING IN MIDFIELD

Midfield players need to be all-rounders. They have to support the defence when needed, but they must also be good in attack. 'Anchors' and 'wing backs' are two kinds of midfielder with particular roles in defence.

Main area of responsibility for wing backs:

★ *Typical situation: The wing back works with a full back in the early stages of an attack.*

Together they close down space around the attacker.

Main area of responsibility for anchor:

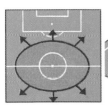

★ *Typical situation: the anchor takes on a midfield challenge while the defenders run back into position.*

The 'anchor' links the backs and midfield players.
★ You must be able to jockey, challenge and attack.

★ You must be able to read the game in front and behind you and give support wherever it is needed.

Wing backs help challenge attacks on the wing.
★ You must be good at covering for defenders and giving support.
★ You must be fit and fast and be a good dribbler.

For a link to a website about the defensive positions of a soccer team, go to **www.usborne-quicklinks.com**

DEFENDING AT CORNERS

Corners are one of the most dangerous situations for a defending team. Your opponents have quite a high chance of scoring, so you need to be clear about what each player is going to do and be very disciplined in carrying out your tactics.

KEY POSITIONS

Think about what your opponents might try. Some moves are often used. One is swinging the ball in close to the near post, and another is swinging it out for a key attacker to head at goal. Prepare by placing your best players in the danger areas.

One reliable defender should support the goalkeeper by covering the far post.

The goalkeeper should stand in front of the far post to see the goal and penalty area.

One defender should cover the near post, but without blocking the goalkeeper's view.

Attackers often aim for the near post because it is hard for the goalkeeper to reach.

Watch out for attackers who are good at coming in and heading.

Make sure you have central defenders who are good at heading and not afraid to challenge.

CORNER RULES

There are two main rules which make a difference to defending at corners:
★ Remember that an attacker cannot be offside from a direct corner kick.
★ All defenders have to keep a distance of 9m (30ft) from the player taking the corner.

HELPING THE GOALKEEPER

The goalkeeper is usually in charge of the goal area at corners, so listen out for his instructions and don't block his view. This is very important around the near post and goal area.

Here, Belgian goalkeeper Michel Preud'homme reaches for the ball in a match against Morocco.

COVERING SHORT CORNERS

If you see an attacker moving out towards the player taking the corner, your opponents may try a short corner. By making a short pass to another attacker they get a different angle of approach to goal, and they also hope to take your team by surprise.

Watch for the player who takes the corner. He may run round the back of his team-mate.

Two of you can stop this attack by moving forward. Remember the 9m (3ft) rule. You need two players because the player taking the corner will move out as soon as he has done so.

This player moves to cover the player who took the corner.

FILLING IN THE GAPS

Once the key positions are covered, the rest of you must make sure there are no other holes. How you do this will depend on which marking system you use.

If you are marking zonally, the team spreads out evenly over the penalty area. Each player should cover the area in front of him.

In a real situation, there would be many more attackers in the areas filled by the arrows.

If you are marking man-to-man, you should get goal-side of your opponent and stick with him as he tries to find space to run into.

The attackers may use most of their players.

ATTACKING THE BALL

When you are all in place and the corner is taken, you must all stay alert and make sure you are first to the ball to get it out of danger. As long as you challenge fairly, you don't need to worry about bumping into other players.

Here, Gareth Southgate and Paul Ince, playing in the England team, challenge for the ball together in a match against Switzerland.

For a link to a website with helpful game advice from a professional goalkeeper, go to **www.usborne-quicklinks.com**

FREE KICKS AND THROW-INS

Any dead ball situation that is awarded against you gives your opponents an advantage. Having gained possession, they will try to create good shooting opportunities, especially in your defending third. You need to keep alert and disciplined.

As the throw is taken, defenders move into goal-side positions.

DEFENDING AT THROW-INS

This player is not offside. A player cannot be offside from a direct throw-in.

Your opponents will take the throw-in as quickly as they can, so don't lose concentration and don't stop moving. Use the time to move into a stronger goal-side position.

Mark any player who is likely to receive the throw. Someone should mark the thrower so that he can't run into space after the throw.

Beware of long throws in the defending third. Treat them like corners (see pages 26-27).

INDIRECT FREE KICKS

When an indirect free kick is awarded against you, you must go back 9m (30ft) from the ball. Your opponents cannot shoot directly at goal - another player has to touch the ball first. This means that as soon as the kick is taken, you can move in to close down the gap before an opponent shoots.

In or near the penalty area you can form a wall (see opposite). Be ready to move very quickly.

Direction of play

Here, the kick has been taken, so defenders run towards the ball.

DIRECT FREE KICKS

A direct free kick allows opponents a direct shot at goal. In your defensive third, you need a defensive wall to block the shot. This should cover as much of the goal as possible without blocking the goalkeeper's view, and must be 9m (30ft) from the kick. You should also move plenty of other players into the penalty area.

BUILDING A WALL

Watch the ball by lifting your eyes, not your head.

You must form the wall quickly.

Line up in order of height. The tallest player stands in front of the post furthest from the goalkeeper.

Everyone in the wall should stand very close to the player next to him so that there aren't any gaps.

Protect your head by tucking it down on your chest, and place your hands over your genitals.

CENTRAL KICKS

If the kick is in front of the goal, you will need up to five players in the wall. Line up so that the goalkeeper has a view of the ball.

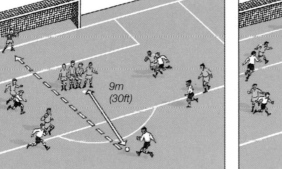

9m (30ft)

KICKS FROM THE SIDE

If the kick is to the side of the goal, it is more likely that the kicker will try to cross the ball to another attacker.

9m (30ft)

Other players should mark attackers man-to-man, but also keep a good view of the ball.

The wall must hold firm as the kick is taken, then move quickly to follow up any rebounds.

Here, you only need two or three players in the wall. The rest of you should spread out.

As soon as the kick is taken, everyone must move towards the ball quickly to clear it out of danger.

For links to websites where you can find out about free kicks and throw-ins, go to **www.usborne-quicklinks.com**

DEFENCE INTO ATTACK

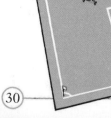

The most important aim when you are playing a game of football is to win. Stopping the other team from scoring is one half of this, but even if you are playing in a defensive position you should be thinking about the other half of your aim – to attack and score goals.

GETTING AN OVERVIEW

Your overall attitude when you are in defence is essential for your success. If your team falls apart as soon as you lose possession, the other team will probably win. Always believe that you can win the ball back, and be ready to attack again.

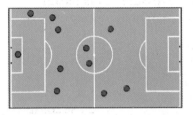
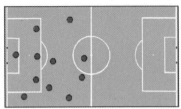
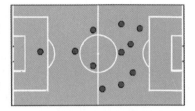

1. This team is in a weak position. It is spread out, leaving lots of holes. This makes it difficult to work together and push forward.

2. This team is in a much stronger position. Although it is in its defending third, the team can communicate and send the ball forward.

3. This team is in a strong position, too. Although there is a lot of space behind the defence, the attackers will find it hard to move into it.

DEFENDING FROM THE BACK

The second position above shows a team defending from the back. This means that you all drop back into your half when the other team gains possession. This can fool attackers in a number of ways.

By dropping back, you give the other team a false sense of success. They may make mistakes.

Dropping back gives you time to regroup, fill in spaces and attack on your own terms.

Once you regain possession of the ball in your own half, your whole team can move up together and build a solid attack.

DEFENDING FROM THE FRONT

Defending from the front, (see the third picture, left) means holding your ground when the other team gain possession in their own third. It is a positive way to defend, giving you a strong attacking position if you regain possession.

Your defence goes back no further than the half-way line. This gives the attackers very little space to move forward and puts them under a lot of pressure. This means that you are likely to regain possession.

Your opponents, especially their goalkeeper, may try sending the ball over you. If they do, mark all attackers tightly to make it difficult for them to reach the ball.

The defenders can reach the goalkeeper's long ball before the attackers can get to it.

SUMMARY AND REMINDER TIPS

★ Always stay in a goal-side position from your opponent.

★ Delay your opponents as much as you can by jockeying.

★ Watch your man when you are marking. Don't let yourself be distracted.

★ When challenging for the ball, put your whole body into it.

★ Learn to clear the ball with strong headers and lofted drives.

★ Play wisely in your defending third. Don't take silly risks.

★ Concentrate when the ball goes out of play. Use the time to get into position.

★ As a team, close down the space and options open to opponents.

★ Make sure you understand your team formation and your position in it.

★ Above all, think positively and keep working as a team, so that when you gain possession you are in a strong position to launch an attack.

For links to websites with the latest news about soccer leagues around the world, go to **www.usborne-quicklinks.com**

INDEX

If you would like to improve your soccer by attending a soccer course
in your holidays, you can find out about different courses from:

Bobby Charlton International Ltd
Hopwood Hall, Rochdale Road
Middleton, Manchester M24 6XH
Tel: 0161 643 3113

Answers to the quiz on page 23:
1) Offside (the offside player receives the ball indirectly from the throw-in) 2) Not offside (the offside player is not
interfering with play) 3) Offside (he is in a position which gives him an advantage) 4 Not offside (he dribbles through).

This edition first published in 2007 by Usborne
Publishing Ltd., 83-85 Saffron Hill, London
EC1N 8RT, England. www.usborne.com
Copyright © 1996, 2003, 2007 Usborne Publishing Ltd.